# MYSTERIES OF THE ROSARY FOR CHILDREN AND THE YOUNG AT HEART

# MYSTERIES OF THE ROSARY

## FOR CHILDREN AND THE YOUNG AT HEART

CHERYL RYBARCZYK

Xulon Press

Xulon Press
2301 Lucien Way #415
Maitland, FL 32751
407.339.4217
www.xulonpress.com

Unless otherwise indicated, Direct Quotes are from the St. Joseph Edition of the New American Bible, Copyright 1992. All rights reserved. Used by permission.

Printed in the United States of America.

ISBN-13: 978-1-5456-6578-7

# DEDICATION

I dedicate this devotional first and foremost to Jesus and His Blessed Mother. Additionally, I dedicate this book to my grandsons Keith, Conor, Colin, Finn, Lochlan, Tierney, and Benneit as well as Kaden and Keehan. Finally, I dedicate this project to all of my former grade school and high school students.

# Acknowledgements

Thank you to my sister, Marilyn Westerberg, for encouraging me to have this devotional published. I also thank her for her input and suggestions.

Thank you to my son-in-law, Jason Gedmin, for his technical expertise. Without his help this project could not have been completed.

Thank you to my very good friend, Betsy Quas, for proof-reading my manuscript and offering suggestions for improvement.

Thank you to my daughter Karli Gedmin, for her encouragement and support throughout this endeavor.

# TABLE OF CONTENTS

# INTRODUCTION

H ave you ever wanted to get closer to Jesus? What better way could you do so than by concentrating on His life and the sacrifice He made for you. This book will help you to focus on the birth, life, death and resurrection of Jesus as you pray traditional Catholic prayers. Following are instructions for praying the rosary and meditating on the life of Christ. May this devotional fill you with a greater love for Jesus Christ and an appreciation for all He has done for you.

## Instructions for praying the rosary

1. Begin by saying the Apostles Creed on the Cross.

2. On the first bead, pray the Our Father.

3. On each of the next three beads, pray a Hail Mary.

4. Finish the introductory prayers with the Glory Be prayer.

5. Next, turn to the Mysteries you will focus on for that day. Read the meditation for the first mystery. Then recite the Our Father on the first single bead that starts the decade. After reciting the Our Father, say a Hail Mary on each of the next ten beads (the first decade). As you recite each Hail Mary, think about the mystery you have just read and its importance in the life of Jesus. At the end of the ten Hail Marys, recite the Glory Be to end the decade. Repeat these steps for each of the next four decades, always using the meditation to guide your thoughts.

## Order of the Mysteries

Joyful Mysteries.........Monday and Saturday

Sorrowful Mysteries.........Tuesday and Friday

Glorious Mysteries.........Wednesday and Sunday

Luminous Mysteries.........Thursday

# THE
# JOYFUL MYSTERIES

# THE FIRST JOYFUL MYSTERY
## The Annunciation

The angel Gabriel was sent by God
To Mary His chosen one,
Who would soon become the mother
Of His only begotten Son.

"Dear Mary," the angel said,
"With God you have found favor,
"And soon from your blessed womb
"Shall come the promised Savior.

"And this child that you shall conceive
"Will be called Son of the Most High.
"By name will be known as Jesus
"On this message you may rely.

"He will rule the house of Jacob,
"And his kingdom will have no end.
"I am conveying this to you
"That you may listen and attend."

Mary then said to the angel,
"I do not know how this can be;
"For to serve my God completely,
"I have promised Him chastity."

"Do not be concerned, dear Mary;
"God's great love overshadows you.
"By means of the Holy Spirit,
"What is foretold will soon come true."

"The child you bear will be called holy,
For the Son of God He will be."
And though this news was amazing,
Mary accepted it faithfully.

"May it be done unto me," she said,
"According to your word."
For Mary trusted at once
Everything she had seen and heard.

# THE SECOND JOYFUL MYSTERY
## The Visitation

When Gabriel told Mary
To Jesus she would give birth,
He brought another message
From heaven unto earth.

"Your dear cousin Elizabeth
"Will also deliver a son;
"And this long awaited child
"Will precede the anointed One."

To a hill town of Judah
The young Mary then did speed.
She hoped to help her cousin
In whatever she might need.

And when Elizabeth's babe
Heard humble Mary say hello,
He jumped for joy inside the womb,
For his love did so overflow.

"Blessed are you among women,"
His mother exclaimed with much joy;
"And blessed is the fruit of your womb,"
For Elizabeth knew of the boy.

Then Mary thus responded
With heartfelt fervor and grace,
A canticle of praise and love
To the God of the whole human race.

"I am just a lowly servant,"
Mary told her cousin and friend.
"The Mighty One has so blessed me,
"I will serve Him until the end."

Thus, with the faith filled Elizabeth
For three months Mary did stay.
She helped do chores and fix meals,
But most of all she did pray.

# The Nativity

As time went by, large with Child
The Virgin Mary ever grew.
Then Joseph left for Bethlehem,
Taking his holy wife, too.

For the two went off to be counted
In the town of their ancestral birth.
Since it was in this quiet little place
That God's Son would be born on earth.

To the little town of David
The Holy Pair arrived one day,
Only to find that nowhere around
Was there a place for them to stay.

"Go to the stable," the innkeeper said,
"At least it is out of the cold."
So Mary and Joseph did what he said,
And found it was just as he told.

The breath of the ox, the
donkey and sheep
Helped keep the young couple warm.
Then far into the eve, just at midnight,
Their Infant child was born.

Suddenly, choirs of angels
Could be heard announcing the birth.
"Glory to God in the highest,
And peace to His people on earth."

Mary knelt and Joseph knelt
To pay homage to the King.
Shepherds came and Wise Men came,
And presents they did bring.

Oh, what a peaceful night it was
With a star shining brightly above.
The long awaited Savior arrived
Because of God's merciful love.

# THE FOURTH JOYFUL MYSTERY
## The Presentation

To the temple in Jerusalem
Mary and Joseph brought their Son.
For the law required consecration,
If a boy was the first-born one.

Jesus was thus presented to God,
Who looked down from heaven above,
And watched as the Holy Family
Offered a sacrifice of turtledoves.

Then Simeon, a holy man,
Hearing Jesus called by name,
Rejoiced when he saw the child,
And thus did firmly proclaim:

"Now, Master, you may take me,
"In peace I wish to go,
"For everything you promised
"Has turned out to be so.

"Whether Jew or Gentile, it matters not
"For this Child will be the light,
"To lead us all to salvation
"That we may be pleasing in your sight."

"You, dear Mary, must be brave
"For a sword will pierce your heart.
"But God's love is ever steadfast;
"From Him you never will part."

Then Anna, too, a prophetess,
Upon the Holy Family came.
She gave thanks to God for this Child
And prayed that all would
know His name.

Thus Anna spread the word to all
Announcing the time of salvation.
For Jesus, the Savior, had come to earth
To redeem each and every nation.

# THE FIFTH JOYFUL MYSTERY
## The Finding of Jesus in the Temple

When the child Jesus was
twelve years old
With his parents to the temple He went,
To celebrate the feast of Passover
Which was always a joyous event.

For this feast allowed the Jewish people
To ponder their slavery and recall
How Yahweh delivered them from
their plight
By freeing them one and all.

But when this festival was over,
And Mary and Joseph headed home,
They soon discovered to their dismay
That they were very much alone.

They searched for Jesus among the
travelers,
But sadly, it was to no avail.
They then returned to Jerusalem,
Returning along the same worn trail.

On the third day they reached the temple,
And were relieved by what they did find.
For there stood Jesus among the teachers
Asking them questions of every kind.

All who heard him were greatly amazed
At the brilliance and depth of his speech.
He seemed to know as much,
maybe more,
Than the very ones who did teach.

Even his parents were awestruck
And asked him without further ado,
"Son, why have you done this to us?
"We've been so worried about you."

"Why were you looking for me?" he asked.
"But perhaps you do not understand,
"That in my father's house I must be,
"Always obedient to his command."

But Mary and Joseph kept quiet,
Not understanding what He said.
For they knew their Son was different,
And by the Holy Spirit He was led.

To Nazareth the Family returned,
Where Jesus grew in wisdom and grace,
Becoming pleasing in all that He did,
To God and the whole human race.

# THE
# LUMINOUS MYSTERIES

# The First Luminous Mystery
## The Baptism of Jesus

Before Jesus began his public ministry,
Another was chosen to prepare the way.
A humble man named John the Baptizer
Reformed many people by what
he did say.

His own simple life was a lesson for all.
He only partook of locust and honey.
He wore camel hair clothing and a
leather belt,
Which for him were worth far more
than money.

His message of repentance was
heard by many.
They began to think the Savior
he might be.
John brought them to confess their sins,
And assured them the Messiah
was not he.

John told the crowd, "I baptize you
with water,
"But He will baptize with fire and
the Spirit.
"I am not worthy to carry His sandals,"
Which news truly amazed those who
did hear it.

Then Jesus Himself came to be
baptized by John,
At which time an amazing
miracle occurred.
The Spirit of God came upon Him
like a dove.
The heavens opened and a voice
was heard.

God confirmed all that John had
been teaching.
He recognized Jesus as His only
begotten Son.
John was thus encouraged to continue
his mission
Of preaching repentance to each and
every one.

# THE SECOND LUMINOUS MYSTERY
## The Wedding Feast at Cana

After leaving His town of Nazareth,
Jesus went to Cana in Galilee.
Invited to a wedding there
Were His mother, His disciples and He.

His mother ever concerned for others,
Realized the servers were filled
with dread.
The wine refreshment had run out,
And there were more people to be fed.

She quickly sought out her Son Jesus.
"They have no wine," she thus implored.
"Woman, how does your concern
affect me?
"My hour has not yet come,"
said the Lord.

"Do whatever he tells you," she said
To the servers who quickly complied.
For they wanted to spare
embarrassment
To the happy young groom and his bride.

So Jesus then ordered the
servants nearby
To fill six jars with water to the brim.
The servants did as Jesus had asked
Then turned for instructions from him.

"Draw some and take it to the
headwaiter,"
Jesus told them as he watched from afar.
For something miraculous
had happened
To the water that had been in the jar.

It had turned to wine and the
headwaiter said
To the groom he had called over his way,
"I'm amazed you saved the best
wine for last
And served the lesser wine earlier today."

Thus this was the first miracle of Jesus,
Performed in Cana to reveal His glory.
His disciples began believing in Him,
But this was just the start of His story.

# THE THIRD LUMINOUS MYSTERY
## Proclamation of the Gospel

When Jesus heard that John had
been arrested,
He withdrew to the area of Galilee.
He went to live in the town of Capernaum,
Which was situated by the sea.

"Repent for the kingdom of God is at hand,"
Was the message He preached
far and wide.
He cured the sick, the blind and the lepers
With His Twelve Apostles by His side.

"Man must be born again of water
and Spirit,
"If in the Kingdom of God, he wishes to be,
"And to accept the kingdom as a
child does,"
Were the words of Jesus's most
humble plea.

For Jesus came to call the world's sinners
To reject Satan and sin and proclaim
mercy for all.
He delivered a holy Sermon on the Mount
To listeners who would respond to His call.

"Love your enemies, pray for your
persecutors,"
Jesus did entreat the people
gathered around.
And all who heard were amazed at
the wisdom,
Upon which this prophet and teacher
did expound.

Jesus said, "Blessed are those
who are meek,
"Inheriting the Kingdom will be their gift,
"And blessed are those who show mercy
"For mercy itself will their souls uplift."

"Blessed are those doing all good deeds,
"With their rewards, they will be satisfied.
"For God is pleased with righteous living,
"And His generosity will not be denied."

To ensure that the people remembered
His words,
Jesus chose Peter to lead in His name.
For whatever he bound and
loosed on earth,
Would be bound and loosed in
heaven the same.

# THE FOURTH LUMINOUS MYSTERY
## The Transfiguration

Jesus took Peter, James and his
brother John
Up to the top of a mountain so high.
There a wondrous event did occur;
The importance of which we cannot deny.

For Jesus was transformed before them,
The clothes He wore became
dazzling white.
His face was as brilliant as the sun,
And His Apostles were amazed at
this sight.

Moses and Elijah appeared
with Him, too,
Discussing the Passion Jesus would
soon face.
But the Apostles did not yet
understand that
Jesus would die to save the whole
human race.

Peter, knowing something significant
was occurring,
And being amazed began to say,
"Rabbi, let us build one tent for
each of you,"
But was stopped in an unusual way.

For behold, a bright cloud cast a shadow
over them,
And a voice came out of the
cloud and said,
"This is My Beloved Son, listen to Him,"
Whereupon the men fell to the ground
as though dead.

For they were terrified when they heard
the voice,
Afraid to look up at what they might see.
They did not yet understand that
Jesus is Lord
For He wanted to instruct these
favored three.

He cautioned them to say nothing of
the vision
Until after He had risen from the dead.
For many amazing events would occur
Before they would understand what He
had done and said.

So, they kept the matter to themselves,
Questioning what rising from the
dead did mean;
But it wouldn't be until some time later
That they would speak about what
they had seen.

# THE FIFTH LUMINOUS MYSTERY
## The Institution of the Eucharist

On the occasion of the Passover feast,
Jesus and His Apostles
gathered together.
He wanted to share one last meal
with them
Before He would be made to suffer.

He sent Peter and John to the house
of a friend
Who agreed to provide a place for
them to dine.
It was here that something miraculous
Would happen to the bread and the wine.

Jesus told His Apostles something
disturbing
As they sat around the dinner table.
He said one of them would betray Him.
Of this no one thought he was able.

As the meal progressed, Jesus took
bread in His hands.
Giving thanks, He raised it to His
Father above.
He blessed, broke and passed it to
His Apostles.
"Take and eat; this is my body," He said
with great love.

When the meal was finished, Jesus
took the cup,
And giving thanks, He gave it to
them and said,
"This is my blood of the new covenant,
"For the forgiveness of sins, it
must be shed."

Thus this was the first celebrated Mass,
Which continues to be observed
every day,
Where the true presence of the Lord
Is received by us in this way.

# The
# Sorrowful Mysteries

# THE FIRST SORROWFUL MYSTERY
## The Agony in the Garden

When the Last Supper was over
At the end of a very long day,
Jesus took his Apostles to Gethsemene,
With Him he hoped they would pray.

He took aside Peter, James and John,
And with much sorrow in His heart,
He told them of His great sadness,
And of how He would soon have to part.

He said to His favored Apostles,
"Stay here and watch with me as I pray."
But their eyes grew heavy with sleep.
And soon they were nodding away.

Jesus moved a short distance from them,
And He fell with His face to the ground.
There He prayed to His Father in heaven
In the silence that seemed to abound.

"My Father, if it is possible,
"May this cup be taken from me;
"Yet not as I will, but as you will,"
Were the words of His most loving plea.

An angel then appeared to Him
To wipe His face of blood and sweat.
Though this brought Him some comfort,
His agony was not over, yet.

He then returned to His disciples,
Their repose made Him feel rather bleak.
"Watch and pray," he said, "not to
be tested,
"The spirit is willing, but the
flesh is weak."

He prayed once again to His Father,
Asking that the cup be taken away.
But He knew no matter what happened,
Complete obedience would He display.

Alas, Jesus said to His disciples,
"Are you still sleeping and taking
your rest?
"The hour has come; my
betrayer is here."
For Judas had not withstood the test.

# THE SECOND SORROWFUL MYSTERY
## The Scourging at the Pillar

The chief priests and elders brought
Jesus forth,
Early in the morning of that fateful day.
In chains they took him to Pontius Pilate,
"Condemned to death," they hoped
Pilate would say.

At that time the betrayer named Judas,
Aware of what had become Jesus's fate,
And deeply regretting his
dreadful actions,
Took his life, thinking repentance too late.

As Jesus stood before Pontius Pilate,
He asked, "Are you the king of
the Jews?"
"It is as you say," Jesus replied.
Though many did not agree with
this news.

The chief priests accused Jesus unfairly;
Pilate knew Jesus had done
nothing wrong.
He sensed that it was out of envy
The crowd had become an unruly throng.

To satisfy their unjust anger,
And on the occasion of their feast,
Pilate offered to free a prisoner,
Hoping Jesus would then be released.

But the crowd had chosen another;
Not wanting Jesus to be freed.
"Crucify Him," they kept demanding,
For they were filled with hatred indeed.

Pilate washed his hands of the affair.
"Look to it yourselves," he then replied.
"His blood be on us and our children,"
The angry crowd violently cried.

The soldiers then tied Jesus to a pillar
Where he was whipped in a very
cruel way;
But Jesus bore His pain with dignity,
Never a condemning word would He say.

# THE THIRD SORROWFUL MYSTERY
## The Crowning of Thorns

Jesus was led into the Praetorium;
The taunting soldiers he had to face.
There he was subjected to much torture,
Of compassion, there was not a trace.

One by one they jeered at the Savior;
A robe of purple they put on His back.
In His right hand they placed a reed,
Thus to mock Him alas and alack.

They twisted together a crown of thorns,
Which they then cruelly placed
on His head.
They knelt down and worshiped
before Him;
"Hail, King of the Jews," they
mockingly said.

They spit upon Him and laughed at Him.
They were demons in the guise of men.
They took their staffs and
struck His head,
Over and over again.

Then having finished with their
devilish sport,
They stripped Him of the purple robe
once more.
Into His own clothes they made
Him redress,
These men who were rotten to the core.

Though Jesus suffered much at
their hands,
This was just the beginning of his strife.
There would be no satisfying their anger
Until they had stripped Jesus of his life.

Yet, Pilate attempted one last time
To get the crowd to set Jesus free.
But their hearts were so filled
with hatred
That he knew this could never be.

Since Pilate was a coward at heart,
To kill Jesus, he did not think was a loss.
So to save face and protect his power,
He condemned Jesus to die on
the cross.

# THE FOURTH SORROWFUL MYSTERY
## The Carrying of the Cross

Pilate sentenced Jesus to death on
the cross,
Though he knew our Lord had done
nothing wrong.
Onto His shoulder, Jesus lifted the wood
As the crowd pushed and shoved
Him along.

Three times as He struggled with
His burden,
Our Savior stumbled and fell to
the ground.
Amidst jeers and shoves from the
angry crowd,
He was alone with not a friend
to be found.

His mother Mary followed closely,
Shedding tears to see her son
so abused.
Yet she accepted all things
God ordained;
Nothing He asked had she ever refused.

The weight of the cross and His injuries
Were almost more than Our Savior
could bear.
So, the soldiers seized Simon
of Cyrenne
To help Jesus in this wretched affair.

Though consumed with much
sorrow and pain,
Jesus never forgot the faithful few.
To Jerusalem's women whom He loved,
He spoke words of courage and
comfort, too.

At last the sad procession of people
With our dear Lord reached the top
of the hill,
Where Jesus was stripped of
His garments,
Thereby the prophecy they did fulfill.

# The Fifth Sorrowful Mystery
## The Crucifixion

Jesus's body was nailed to the cross
As onlookers heard Him cry out in pain.
The cross was then lifted high
above ground;
To crucify our Lord seemed quite insane.

Above Jesus's head, Pilate had
words written,
"Jesus the Nazorean, King of the Jews."
The chief priests protested this
inscription,
But Pilate kept it, ignoring their views.

As Jesus hung there with two sinful men,
One of them repented before he died.
"Paradise is your reward," Jesus said,
As the good thief bowed his head
and cried.

To His mother Mary and His friend John,
Jesus had these words of pure
love to say,
"You are now his mother and he
your son,"
And they cared for each other from
that day.

To His sheepfold, too, Jesus gave
much thought,
"Father, forgive them, they know not
what they do,"
And thus He submitted to His
father's will,
Sacrificing Himself for me and for you.

Then Jesus cried out giving up His spirit,
As darkness enveloped the entire place.
Thereby fulfilling His Father's mission
Of dying to save the whole human race.

# THE
# GLORIOUS MYSTERIES

# THE FIRST GLORIOUS MYSTERY
## The Resurrection

On that first Easter morning
At the very break of day,
The women who loved Jesus
Joined together and did say,

"Let us go to Jesus' tomb
"To anoint His head and feet."
Arriving there, however,
Two men in white they did meet.

In fact, these men were angels who
Spoke gently to the women and said,
"Look for Jesus among the living,
"You will not find Him among the dead."

Overwhelmed by what they heard,
To the Apostles the women did speed.
Though they told their story to everyone,
The news was not well received.

Peter and John ran back to the tomb.
It was empty just as the women said.
Only the linen strips were left behind
That had covered Jesus's
body and head.

Then Mary, who had followed the men,
Watched as Peter and John
walked away.
She was weeping great tears of sadness
When suddenly she heard a man say,

"Woman, why are you crying like that?
"Who is it you are looking for?"
"Tell me where my Lord is," she said,
"That I just might see Him once more."

Then ever so softly and gently,
The man called the woman by name.
"Mary," he said with such compassion,
That her heart with love burst aflame.

"Teacher," she replied in recognition.
For it was Jesus her Savior and Lord.
He had risen from the dead as he said;
With the Scriptures this was in accord.

"Go to my brothers and tell them
"That before them I go to Galilee.
"It is there that I will await them,
"So that they might see and
believe in me."

# THE SECOND GLORIOUS MYSTERY
## The Ascension

After Jesus rose from the dead,
To two disciples he did appear.
Though it was a surprise to these men,
They never did experience fear.

They hurried instead to the Apostles
To give witness to what they had seen.
"The Lord has appeared to us," they said,
"To explain what His death did mean."

The Apostles were confused
and puzzled.
They didn't seem to know what to do.
Suddenly Jesus appeared before them
Saying warmly, "Peace be unto you."

"For I have come to fulfill the promise
"Made by My Father in heaven above.
"But first you must all spread
the message
"Of what I have done for you out of love."

Jesus then instructed His Apostles
Now and again for the next forty days,
Helping them to understand
their mission
And promising to be with them always.

"Go into the world and proclaim
the gospel,"
Jesus urged His disciples to obey.
"Signs will accompany those
who believe,"
And He told them many other
things that day.

Then finally He took them to Bethany.
He lifted His hands, blessed them
and said,
"I go before you now into heaven,
"But my Spirit will be with you instead."

Jesus was taken up into heaven
Where He remains with the Father
'til that day,
When all the faithful will join Him forever,
And His kingdom will never fade away.

# The Descent of the Holy Spirit Upon the Apostles and the Blessed Mother

Fifty days after that first Easter morn
And gathered together in one place,
Were Mary, the Apostles and others,
Who were filled with God's special grace.

Suddenly could be heard a violent wind,
Which filled the whole house where
they stayed.
They gathered round the dinner table,
Raised their eyes to heaven and prayed.

Then what looked like flames or
tongues of fire,
Separated and came to rest on each,
Filling them with the gifts of the spirit,
Particularly the gift of speech.

For all who spoke of Jesus the Savior,
Though their native tongues
weren't the same,
Were understood by all who listened
No matter from what nation they came.

This perplexed and amazed the listeners,
As they questioned how this event
came to be.

Then Peter raised his hand for
their silence,
As he explained about this prophecy.

Peter said, "I will pour out my Spirit,
"God told the people through the
prophet Joel.
"I will show wonders in the
heavens above,
"And there will be signs on the
earth below."

The people were told to stop sinning,
"Repent and be baptized each
one of you.
"Ask Jesus to forgive your sinful ways,
"Then the Holy Spirit will come upon
you, too."

Now the people who heard this
were amazed
At the many things Peter had to say.
Those who accepted were
soon baptized,
And many faithful were added that day.

# THE FOURTH GLORIOUS MYSTERY
## The Assumption of Mary

Mary, the Blessed Mother of Jesus,
In virtues and many graces had grown,
Taken care of by the Apostle John
Who had welcomed her into his home.

From there she humbly served God
the Father,
Responding to whatever He did ask.
This she did throughout her lifetime,
Never once did she refuse any task.

Mary's life was an example to all
Of how to lovingly serve the Lord.
Her Spirit rejoiced in God her Savior
Of this the Scriptures do record.

She knew the Lord had done great
things for her.
She acknowledged and praised His
holy name.
She spent her life giving service to God;
If only we would learn to do the same.

In time Mary's longing to see her Son
Was the thought uppermost in her mind.
God knew the desire of her heart
And would answer her soon, she
would find.

God then responded to Mary's request
To be united to her loving son.
He took her to heaven body and soul;
Her service to Him on earth being done.

# THE FIFTH GLORIOUS MYSTERY

## The Crowning of Mary Queen of Heaven and Earth

Imagine the meeting between these two,
Jesus, the Lord, and His Blessed Mother.
With what joy He must have greeted her
And how they must have embraced
each other.

No doubt choirs of angels were there,
Singing praises to God up above,
And welcoming home His
mother so dear
With joyful songs of everlasting love.

Mary stepped before the throne
of her God
For the first time seeing Him face to face,
The love between them was so
profound that
Mary's heart overflowed with
much grace.

Then God placed her next to her Son's
right side,
And put a crown of jewels
upon her head.
He named her Queen of
Heaven and Earth
And of all those who are living or dead.

Through Mary we come to know
God better.
She pleads to Him for us day and night,
To grant us mercy and forgiveness
Until we become pleasing in His sight.

Mary never forgets those of us,
Who to the earth are still bound.
Ever encouraging the prayer of
the rosary,
Where true love and peace may
be found.

# About the Author

Cheryl Rybarczyk is a retired school teacher having taught mostly in Catholic Schools. Praying the rosary was an important part of her own childhood, and she encouraged her grade school students to develop the practice. She wrote the initial three sets of Mysteries for her students to help them focus as they prayed. She later added the Luminous Mysteries. At her sister's encouragement, she readied the devotional for publication for children and anyone who would benefit from a simple and effective meditation on the life and sacrifice of our Lord Jesus Christ.

CPSIA information can be obtained
at www.ICGtesting.com
Printed in the USA
BVHW010801120821
614094BV00014B/310